Working Hard to Help

CONTENTS

NATIONAL GEOGRAPHIC | Hampton-Brown

School Publishing

Words with **ar**

Look at each picture. Read the words.

ar

Example:

arm

c**ar**

j**ar**

y**ar**n

c**ar**d

sh**ar**k

High Frequency
Words

High Frequency Words
another
began
buy
children
found
get
just
old
school
together

Key Words

Look at the picture. Read the sentences.

Yard Sale

1. These **children** wanted to **get together** to help their **school**.
2. They **found old** things and **began** to sell them.
3. A man found **just** one pot he wanted to **buy**.
4. He did not want **another** pot!

Which thing would you buy? Why?

Phonics Games
NGReach.com

3

Star Team

by Mark Gaines

Tyler

Can you help a kid who is far, far away, in another part of the world?

Yes, if you're part of a team.

Just look at Tyler Page!

children fishing in Ghana, Africa

In 2007, Tyler was ten. He was watching TV with his mom. Tyler found out about kids who had a hard life. They didn't go to school. These kids had to work.

The "fishing children" are mostly boys age 5 to 14.

They were called "fishing children." They
would march hundreds of miles to a lake.
Then they would set out nets and catch fish
all day long.

Tyler found out it would take $240 to help one kid. But he wanted to help lots of kids. Tyler began to plan how to get money. He started with a car wash.

a car wash

Tyler knew he needed help. He was smart.
He asked his teacher and classmates to help
him. Three weeks after that, they had a car
wash in the school parking lot.

Tyler's class raised $1,175! That would help 4.7 kids. But Tyler had to help that fifth kid, too. He needed $70. A man wanted to help. He gave Tyler's mom a card. Inside was $500!

Tyler and his mom at their lemonade stand

Tyler and his classmates kept raising money. They had more car washes. They set up lemonade stands. They held yard sales.

a yard sale

Yard sales are fun ways to raise cash. A few people get together. They sell old things they don't need. They don't charge much. Others come and buy things because they're cheap.

Tyler and kids buying lemonade at one of Tyler's lemonade stands

Tyler and his classmates worked hard. They raised $38,000 that school year. Other kids wanted to help. So Tyler and five children started Kids Helping Kids.

This team keeps working to save the "fishing children." It also raises money for other children who need help. Hundreds of kids are now part of Kids Helping Kids. It's a LARGE team!

Kids Helping Kids helped many kids.

The "fishing children" send homemade cards to say thank you to Kids Helping Kids.

So, can you help a kid? Yes! Just be part of a helping team. As Tyler says, "Together as a team, we can do it!" ❖

Words with **ar**

Read these words.

car	tray	shark	star
yarn	jar	rake	scarf

Find words with **ar**. Use letters to build them.

c	a	r

Talk **Together**

Choose words from the box above to ask your partner questions.

Where is the <u>car</u> ?

Here is the <u>car</u> .

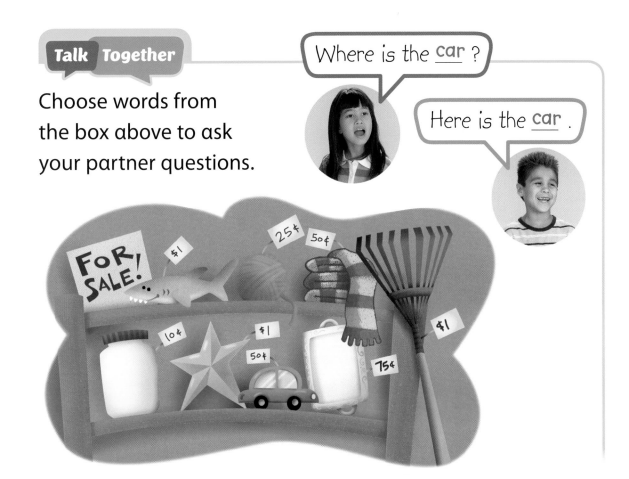

Longer Words with **ar**

ar

Look at each picture. Read the words.

Example:

st**ar**fish

artist

m**ar**ble

p**ar**ty

c**ar**pet

g**ar**den

Words
another
began
buy
children
found
get
just
old
school
together

Key Words

Read the sentences. Match each sentence to something in the picture.

Children Together

1. These **children** like to eat **together** in **school**.
2. This child **just** wanted to **buy** an apple.
3. This child went to **get another** chair.
4. He **found** an **old** chair.
5. He sat and they all **began** to eat.

What do you think the children are saying?

Phonics Games

NGReach.com

17

Farmers' Markets

by Olivia Lee

It is a sunny day in this city park. Summer is just about over. Where are these people going? They are going to the Farmers' Market.

You can come, too!

farmstand

green beans

eggplant

parsnip

pepper

Look! Rows of farmstands line park paths.
Each has different things to sell. You can
buy fresh green beans and eggplant in that
farmstand. You can get parsnips and peppers in
that farmstand.

plums

mushrooms

Let's step partway inside a farmstand.
You can see cartons filled with plums and
melons and beets. There is a box packed with
mushrooms, and another packed with garlic.

A farmers' market is different from a supermarket, but both need farmers. Farmers plant crops, grow crops, and harvest them when they are ripe. Then farmers sell these crops.

Supermarkets buy what farmers grow, at set prices. The crops are then shipped, maybe from far, far away. To pay for that shipping, supermarkets sometimes have to charge you a high price.

But at a farmers' market, farmers get together and sell the food by themselves. This way, they get more money, and you get fresh food right from farms in your own state.

Farmers' markets are hundreds of years old.
These markets began in the U.S. in the 1600s.
City people found that there was little room in
their tiny backyards. They could not plant big
gardens. They needed to get food from farms.

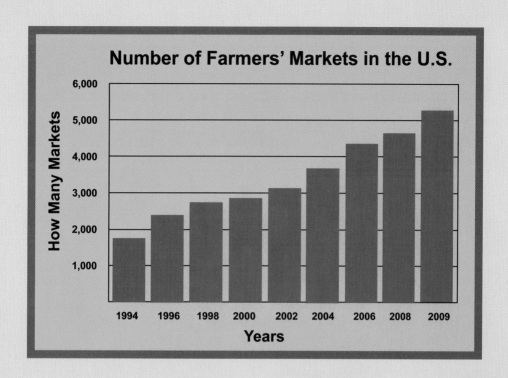

Number of Farmers' Markets in the U.S.

How Many Markets vs *Years*

So farmers close by filled carts with crops. Then they drove their cargo to the city to sell. In the old days, there were just a few farmers' markets. But the number has grown. Just look at this graph!

These days, farmers are teaming up with schools to help children. There are over 1,000 Farm-to-School teams in the U.S. Schools buy fresh food from close groups of farmers.

Farm-to-School teams work best when the crops have just been harvested. In some places, there are crops year round. It is harder in places where most crops are harvested in summer.

When farmers team up, we all win! They can sell their crops at a good price. We can eat fresh food that is good for us. ❖

Longer Words with <u>ar</u>

Read these words.

artist	book	carton	apple
parsnip	starfish	carpet	yardstick

Find words with **ar**.
Use letters to build them.

a	r	t	i	s	t

Talk Together

I found a <u>parsnip</u> and an <u>apple</u>.

Choose words from the box above
to tell your partner what you can
find at this farmers' market.

Who's at the Market?

Look at the picture of a Farmers' Market. Take turns reading the clues and pointing to answers.

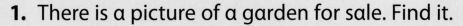

1. There is a picture of a garden for sale. Find it.
2. Some children are marching together. Find them.
3. One farmer is selling jars. Find him.
4. There is a picture of a barn for sale. Find it.
5. A woman wants to buy a bunch of parsnips. Find her.
6. A man just found a large grapefruit. Find him.
7. A woman is standing by an old car. Find her.

Acknowledgments

Grateful acknowledgment is given to the authors, artists, photographers, museums, publishers, and agents for permission to reprint copyrighted material. Every effort has been made to secure the appropriate permission. If any omissions have been made or if corrections are required, please contact the Publisher.

Photographic Credits

CVR (bl) Burke/Triolo Productions/FoodPix/Getty Images. (cr) Catherine Karnow/National Geographic Image Collection. **2** (bl) isgaby/iStockphoto. (br) Jim Workman/National Geographic Image Collection. (cl) Feng Yu/Shutterstock. (cr) Scott Rothstein/Shutterstock. (tr) Tito Wong/ Shutterstock. **3** Liz Garza Williams/Hampton-Brown/National Geographic School Publishing. **4** (c) Victoria Yee. 4-5 (bg) DCD/Shutterstock. **5** (t) Tugela Ridley/epa/Corbis. **6** © IOM 2003 - MGH0012 (Photo: Jean-Philippe Chauzy). **7** (b) Victoria Yee. (tc) Nathan Winter/ iStockphoto. (tl) PhotoDisc/Getty Images. (tr) Artville. **8-9** (tl) Chad Ehlers/Alamy Images. **9** (inset) Tatiana Kopysova/Shutterstock. (t) Adrian Niederhäuser/Shutterstock. **10** Victoria Yee. **11** David Sacks/Lifesize/Getty Images. **12-13** (tl) Victoria Yee. **13** (bl) Estelle/Shutterstock. (cl) Distinctive Images/Shutterstock. (cr) Phil Borges/Danita Delimont Stock Photography. (tr) Distinctive Images/Shutterstock. **14** Phil Borges/Danita Delimont Stock Photography. **15** (c, cr) Liz Garza Williams/Hampton-Brown/National Geographic School Publishing. **16** (bl) Konovalikov Andrey/Shutterstock. (br) Elena Elisseeva/Shutterstock. (cl) Cheryl Casey/ Shutterstock. (cr) Purestock/Getty Images. (tl) Greydon Ludgate/National Geographic Image Collection. (tr) VanHart/Shutterstock. **17** Liz Garza Williams/Hampton-Brown/National Geographic School Publishing. **18** James Lovell/Alamy Images. **19** (cl) MarFot/Shutterstock. (cr) Richard Griffin/Shutterstock. (l) Ivaschenko Roman/Shutterstock. (r) Artville. (t) Angus Oborn/Lonely Planet Images. **20** (cl) Keith Leighton/Alamy Images. (cr) aquariagirl1970/ Shutterstock. (t) Greg Vaughn/Alamy Images. **21** (cl) Gary K Smith/FLPA - Images of Nature/age fotostock. (cr) Denis and Yulia Pogostins/Shutterstock. (tl) Skye Hohmann/Alamy Images. **22** Monkey Business Images/Shutterstock. **23** (cr) Somos/Alamy Images. (t) Frank Vetere/Alamy Images. **24** Prints and Photographs Division, Library of Congress, LC-DIG-nclc-3213. **25** (cl, l, r, cr) Artville. **26** Tim Boyle/Getty Images. **27** (c) R Hamilton Smith/Agstockusa/age fotostock. (tl) Michael Melford/National Geographic Image Collection. (tr) Creatas/age fotostock. **28** (cl) ericlefrancais/Shutterstock. (cr) Image Source/Corbis. (tl) Image Source/Alamy Images. **29** Liz Garza Williams/Hampton-Brown/National Geographic School Publishing.

Illustrator Credits

3, 15, 17, 29 Peter Grosshauer; **30-31** Mattia Cerato

The National Geographic Society

John M. Fahey, Jr., President & Chief Executive Officer
Gilbert M. Grosvenor, Chairman of the Board

Copyright © 2011 The Hampton-Brown Company, Inc., a wholly owned subsidiary of the National Geographic Society, publishing under the imprints National Geographic School Publishing and Hampton-Brown.

National Geographic School Publishing
Hampton-Brown
www.NGSP.com

Printed in the USA.
RR Donnelley, Menasha, WI

ISBN:978-0-7362-8076-1

11 12 13 14 15 16 17 18 19
10 9 8 7 6 5 4 3